LUCKY BAG

The Victoria Wood Song Book

WORDS AND MUSIC BY VICTORIA WOOD

METHUEN

First published in Great Britain in 1984 by Methuen London Ltd 11 New Fetter Lane, London EC4P 4EE
Music by Philip Sparke, Studio Music Company
Design by Christopher Holgate

Text photoset in Palatino by Tek-Art, Croydon, Surrey
Made and printed in Great Britain by Richard Clay (The Chaucer Press) Ltd, Bungay, Suffolk.

ISBN
0 413 56140 2 (hardback)
0 413 56150 X (paperback)

page		
1	Victoria Wood in 'Love Song'	Granada Television
2	Victoria Wood	Capital Press
6	Wood and Walters	Granada Television
8	Victoria Wood	Capital Press
11	'Don't Get Cocky'	Granada Television
15	Julie Walters in 'Living Together'	Granada Television
19	Victoria Wood in 'Thinking of You'	Michael J. Gell
28 – 29	Victoria Wood and Julie Walters in 'Don't Do It'	Granada Television
35	Victoria Wood in 'What We Find'	Michael J. Gell
41	Victoria Wood and Julie Walters in 'Fourteen Again'	Granada Television
47	Victoria Wood in 'Love Song'	Granada Television
51	Paula du Val in 'Nasty Things'	Nick Craney
55	Victoria Wood in 'Song of the Lonely Girl'	Michael J. Gell
59	Victoria Wood in 'I've Had It Up To Here'	Michael Putland
69	Victoria Wood	Arthur Thompson
78	Victoria Wood	Capital Press

LUCKY BAG *Contents*

Victoria Wood, by the woman across the road **7**

Playing the Piano the Victoria Wood way **9**

Don't Get Cocky **11**

Living Together **15**

Thinking of You **19**

Funny How Things Turn Out **23**

Don't Do It **29**

What We Find **35**

Fourteen Again **41**

Love Song **47**

Nasty Things **51**

The Song of the Lonely Girl **55**

I've Had It Up to Here **59**

Bastards **65**

Music and Movement **69**

Northerners **73**

Index **79**

BBC

Victoria Wood, BY THE WOMAN ACROSS THE ROAD

Ooh yes, I've followed Virginia Woolf's career for years. Lovely backhand. Oh, Victoria Wood. She's been going a long time, hasn't she. You should see her first thing in the morning. No, now, 'New Faces' we first saw her on, I remember because our dog was barking and we all said shut up Fluff the lady's doing her best, then it turned out it had its tail up the hoover. She was never off the TV after that, for some time. You'd settle down for a nice serious discussion programme about the rates of vitamins, and there'd be Victoria in a friend's frock, giving us three verses' worth of pertinent ditty. And it wasn't 'That's Life' it was 'Start the Week' on the radio. I suppose a little song in the middle gave Richard Baker a chance to nip out to the doings.

Of course, she was working 'live' as they call it, quite often. Sometimes twice a year. I know one of her fondest memories is being booked as a blue comedienne at an all-male conference. She came off after seven minutes and blames the acoustics.

Well anyway, in 1978 she got some very nice reviews for a little show she did in London called 'In at the Death'. A little comedy thing all about death. There was a girl called Julie Walters in it. They got on quite well. In fact they still do. Anyway, somebody said why don't you write a play, and she thought, why not, it's easier than laying lino. It was called 'Talent'. this play, and they did it at a very nice theatre in Sheffield called the Crucible. Funny name. Well, she nearly went mad with writing plays after that, two more for television, 'Nearly a Happy Ending' and 'Happy Since I Met You', and even a stage musical called 'Good Fun'. She won quite a few awards, which meant borrowing another frock and meeting Princess Margaret, what a business.

Well, you can't write all the year round, because your thumb goes flat, so she went back on the boards. (They only had boards because she'd never laid that lino.) She teamed up with that Spanish magician The Great Soprendo. He liked a laugh, bless him. They went all over with a show called 'Funny Turns'. They toured all over England and Scotland with it, when they decided they should take it to London, because if you live there you need cheering up. Well, they packed them in at the King's Head. No, really, people were passing out. Then it transferred. To the West End. Very posh. Victoria had to buy a new sponge bag.

Anyway, last year Victoria thought she'd do a show on her own. 'Lucky Bag' she called it, which is hardly going to bring the Japanese flocking. The show was just her, by herself. With nobody else there. Not even a fifty piece orchestra. Not even a man with a mouth organ. I thought she'd flipped her boko, but she said it was going to be dead good.

Well, the critics liked it, but then again, they live off halves of mild and never get a square meal so their judgement is bound to be a bit dicky. And then she wrote a film and made a record, so why she hasn't got enough money to line her kitchen curtains, goodness only knows.

And doing another television series. With luck, that won't be on till my evening classes start. Or I might go and have my veins stripped.

And now you tell me there's a book of songs coming out. I suppose if everyone starts singing them it might do the earplug manufacturers a big of good, but I'm dubious.

I shan't buy it. I feel there's too many books in the world. In fact I wrote to Methuen's (and don't tell me there's nothing foreign there) and said don't bother publishing, use the paper for something we can all enjoy, but they seem to be going ahead anyway.

Playing the Piano THE VICTORIA WOOD WAY

I don't play with my left hand. That's the first thing. You can if you want to. We've put some notes in for clever chaps who do want to go bashing away with both hands at the same time, boring everybody stupid. You've probably got a food processor as well, haven't you?

Also, do lots of wrong notes. We haven't written those in, feeling that it's more creative for you to make up your own. We haven't included any raffia, Stanley knives or wholemeal macaroni for the same reason.

Playing the piano, as discussed earlier in my paragraph of the today inst., is quite simple, *viz.*, keep smiling and don't get too much banana sandwich on the black notes. (Doesn't show so much on the white ones, unless the bananas are over-ripe, in which case, reverse the above advice.)

People often ask me about pedals. I say, yes, do get some. Piano pedals are best, but those of you who are dismantling an old moped may find they have an urge to waste not want not. Don't. They don't sound as good, and anyway, they look stupid.

Trills? By all means, but don't blame me if it chips your nail varnish. Also, there is some sort of bother going on about arpeggios. The new Common Market arpeggio is shorter and, I think, not as effective, but this is the price we pay for staying in watching the television when we could have been out voting in a referendum.

Raising the hands very high above the keyboard may get you another couple of bouquets at the end of the concert if you're Vladimir Ashkenazy, (and I don't think you are, are you? He's taller with more of a moody expression,) but it doesn't really help the average ivory tinkler, unless you like painting the ceiling in between chords.

As far as singing goes, you may come a bit of an embarrasing cropper if you're tone deaf or blush easily. We're hoping to publish another book especially for the tone deaf, but it's not the sort of thing a big publishing house will touch, and it may have to be done on the photocopier at the Reference Library (and Heaven only knows how many five pences we'll need, at least twelve I should think).

If you're the sort of person who likes to get drunk and have a sing-song round the piano very late at night, perhaps you'd better move house. And although we certainly do not give permission for these songs to be performed in public, there's bound to be some nit in Bromley who takes no bleeding notice, so here are some performance guidelines. Emphasise every other word, and perform all the others as if they were in 'inverted' 'commas'. I also recommend plenty of winking, pursing of the lips and explanatory gestures of the hands for such words as 'you', 'me', 'I'm buying a bungalow in Weybridge', etc.

Finally, choosing an instrument. Uprights damage less paintwork on the way in, but grands are more useful if you do a lot of dressmaking, or need a flat surface for mixing concrete.

So it's up to you. Some people have found this book very useful, especially those who had trouble with a wobbly wicker plant stand. And I hope you get as much pleasure out of reading this book as I did from the egg and chips with three eggs I had last week. Till then, take care.

We congratulate
You on losing weight.
Don't get cocky, baby,
You're going to be back next month.
We'd say six days' grace
Before you stuff your face,
Don't get cocky baby
You're going to be back next month.

Just take Valerie,
Wouldn't know a calorie
If it came and bit her on the leg.
Starves all day,
And then gives way,
Has eighty bacon butties and a large
fried egg.

You don't play hockey, babe.
You do like Choccy, babe,
So don't get cocky, babe,
You're going to be back next month.

Just take Renée,
Fancied a bikini,
Resisted every snack,
Stripped off in the Bahamas,
Has stretch marks like pyjamas,
Grabbed a bar of chocolate and the
next flight back.

We don't grudge your fun,
We just know it can't be done,
Spurn the spud or ban the bun,
You're going to be back next month.

Take Fiona,
Twenty-seven stoner,
Slimmed herself to bone and specs,
Husband got conjugal,
Threw away his bugle,
Brought her tiny knickers and
demanded sex.

You're a smarty-boots,
We don't give two hoots,
You'll be back in them Crimplene
trouser suits
When you waddle back next month.

Just take Heather,
Her jaws were wired together,
An easy slimming method she had
heard.
Her husband didn't like her skimpy,
Eloped with Wendy from the
Wimpy,
She watched them go and couldn't
say a bleeding word.

Don't Get Cocky

This song is from the television sequel to 'Talent', 'Nearly a Happy Ending'. My character, Maureen, was supposed to have lost three stone at a slimming club and gone out to lose her virginity. I only lost about two stone for the part so we had to do the rest with lots of make-up and a black blazer. The song took place in the Slimming Club, where Maureen is being signed off at target weight (ho ho), and we had a chorus of ladies ranging from the slightly wobbly to the 'Excuse me, who's put a frock on this elephant?' They did a lovely dance routine which was beaten into them by the thinnest choreographer you've ever seen. In fact, you couldn't see her, but you could feel her truncheon.

Don't forget God chose
Those blue eyes, that funny nose,
He made that tissue adipose,
He'll bundle you back next month.

Just take Winnie,
Like a barracks in a pinnie,
Gave up food for Lent.
Her weight loss was fantastic,
But her skin was not elastic.
She's like an inefficient camper in a
creased pink tent.

Still, let's not pretend
There's any decent reason why you
should attend,
It's the only place you'll find a fatter
friend,
You'll have to come back next
month.

All right, skinny, off you sneak,
You can turn the other cheek,
But it's got you out the bloody house
twice a week,
You'll need to come back next month
She will
She'll need to come back next month
Well, this is it
She'll need to come back next
month.

Well, it's the company, basically, isn't
it?

Don't Get Cocky

If it came and bit her on the leg. Starves all day, And
sist - ed eve - ry snack, Stripped off in the Ba-ha - mas, Has
Slimmed her-self to bone and specs, Hus- band got con - ju - gal,
ea - sy slim-ming me - thod she had heard. Her hus-band did - n't like her skim-py, E-loped with
Gave up food for Lent. Her weight loss was fan - tas - tic, But her
Gm D Gm D Gm Fm C7
then gives way, Has eight - y ba - con but- ties and a large fried egg. You
stretch marks like py - ja - mas, Grabbed a bar of choco-late and the next flight back.
Threw a - way his bu - gle, Bought her ti - ny knick-ers and de - mand - ed sex.
Wen - dy from the Wim - py, She watched them go and could-n't say a bleed - ing word.
skin was not e - las - tic. She's like an in - ef - fi - cient camp-er in a creased pink tent.
Fm C7 F7 Bb7
don't play hock - ey, babe. You do like
We don't grudge your fun, We just know it
You're a smar - ty boots, We don't
Don't for - get God chose Those blue eyes, that
Still, let's not pre - tend There's an - y de - cent rea - son why you
Eb Bb7 Eb
Choc - cy babe, So don't get cock - y babe, You'll
can't be done, Spurn the spud or ban the bun, You're
give two hoots, You'll be back in those Crim - plene trou ser suits When
fun - ny nose, He made those tis - sues ad - i - pose, He'll
should at - tend, It's the on - ly place you'll find a fat - ter friend, You'll
Bb7 Eb D° Db7 C7

1.2.3.4
5
have to come back next month.
going to be back next month.
you wad-dle back next month.
bun-dle you back next month.
have to come back next month.
Al-right, skin-ny, off you sneak,
F7 Bb7 Eb D Eb Bb Cm7 Bb Eb Bb7
You can turn the oth-er cheek, But it's got you out the blood-y house twice a week, You'll need to come back next
Eb Bb7 Eb D° Db7 C7 F7 Bb7
(Spoken)
month She will She'll need to come back next month Well, this is it She'll need to come back next
Eb C F7 Bb7 Eb C F7 Bb7
month.
(Spoken) Well, it's the company, basically, isn't it?
Eb Ebdim Fm7 Bb Eb6 Bb7 Eb

Living Together

Living together is great
Living together's like Popeye and
Spinach
Puts hairs on your chest
It's like passing your test
I'm very impressed
Fairly splendid
It's recommended oh.

Living together's a laugh
Living together is ever so matey
It's him in the bath
With you on the loo
The last thing to do
Is worry whether you'll
Stay together but

Ooh in the night in the dark it's so
cosy
All snuggled up nothing left to say
Ooh to intrude any more would be
nosy
Let's slip away, slip away.

Living together is work
Living together's like running a
business
You daren't take a break
You daren't call a halt
It's always your fault
And there's no way of stopping
Production dropping.

Ooh where did all of those moons and
those Junes go?
All the romance of a love that's new
Now it's just 'Who put the knives
where the spoons go?'
Was it you? Was it you?

Living together is mad
Living together's like being in prison
You're never alone
You're sharing a cell
Most days are hell
In addition there's no remission

And ooh in the night you are silently
screaming
Crying for something, you're not sure
what
You hope you might wake up and find
that you're dreaming
But you're not, you're not, you're not.

I wrote this song as part of the soundtrack for a television play called 'Happy Since I Met You'. I wasn't in it, so I hung round in an anorak making a nuisance of myself.

The play was a love story, with fighting. I'm not very good on love, so I banged in a lot of jokes to help out. I didn't put any sex in it – my one concession to dramatic trends was to have the couple sitting up in bed eating cheese and tomato sandwiches.

Living Together

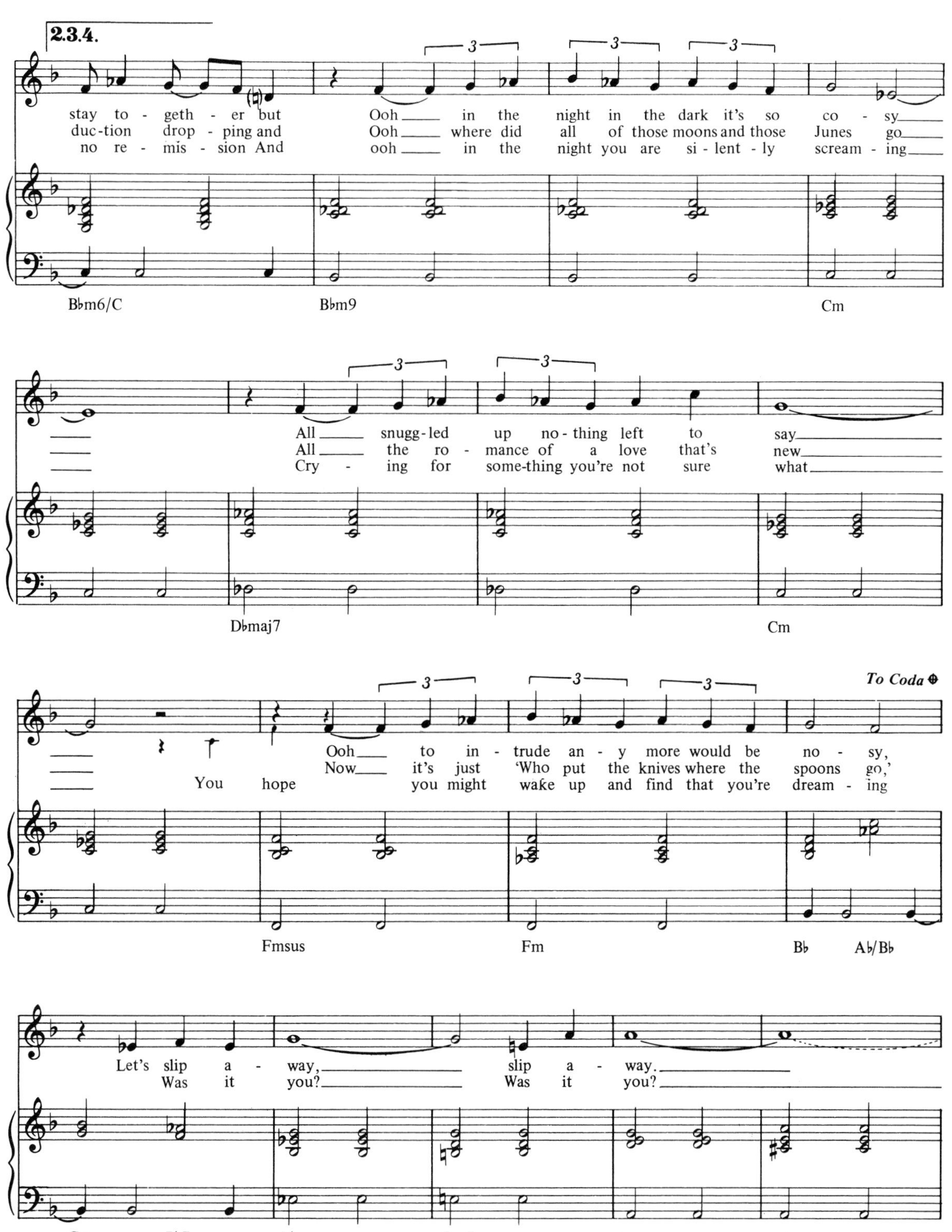
2.3.4.
stay to - geth - er but
duc-tion drop - ping and
no re - mis - sion And
Ooh in the night in the dark it's so co - sy
Ooh where did all of those moons and those Junes go
ooh in the night you are si - lent - ly scream - ing
Bbm6/C
Bbm9
Cm
All snugg - led up no - thing left to say
All the ro - mance of a love that's new
Cry - ing for some-thing you're not sure what
Dbmaj7
Cm
To Coda
You hope
Ooh to in - trude an - y more would be no - sy,
Now it's just 'Who put the knives where the spoons go,'
you might wake up and find that you're dream - ing
Fmsus
Fm
Bb
Ab/Bb
Let's slip a - way, slip a - way.
Was it you? Was it you?
Gm
Bb7
Eb
Em7
Asus
A

1
D.%. (verse 3)
Dm
B♭
Dm
B♭
2
D.%. al Coda (verse 4)
Dm
B♭maj7
Dm
B♭maj7
CODA
But you're not,
you're not,
Gm
B♭7
E♭m
C♭maj7
E♭m
you're not.
ff
C♭maj7
E♭m

Thinking of You

They said our love would never
work
They said that when I met you.
Well they were right, it's over now.
Still, I won't forget you . . . .

When the next door neighbour's
yelling,
When all day I keep on smelling
Old men's macs
Or when my ears are blocked with
wax
When conversation turns to
taxidermy
I will think of you.

When I see a child dismember
Insects, or when I remember
How I feel
The day after an Indian meal
Or when I see a jellied eel
My darling, I will think of you.

Or when my best friend doesn't like
Beryl Cook or David Hockney
Or when I think of Dick Van Dyke
Trying to do a cockney accent.

When the shop is out of Tizer
When above my head there flies a
Jumbo Jet
When all my towels are dripping wet
Or when my pink blancmange won't
set
My darling, I will think of you.

When my aunt says 'Time for shut-
eye',
When I wash up dinner but I
Get no thanks
Whenever I smell septic tanks
Whenever I see two short planks
My darling, I will think of you.

I wrote this for the stage show 'Funny Turns', when it transferred to the Duchess Theatre in 1982. The theatre was sold while we were working there. We came in one day to find our curtains were made of corrugated iron. The best thing about being in the West End is seeing how cross famous people get when they can't find a free meter.

Thinking of You

Moderato
mf
C
F
Fm
rall.
D7
G
They said our love would nev - er work They
C
Fm6
said that when I met you. Well they were right, it's ov - er now. Still, I won't for - get you.
C F G C G+
C
Ab7
D9
G F/G Em/G Dm/G
1. When the next door neigh - bour's yell - ing, When all
2. When I see a child dis - mem - ber In - sects,
3. When the shop is out of Ti - zer When a -
4. When my aunt says, 'Time for shut - eye', When I
C
Cmaj7
Dm7
G
C
Cmaj7

day I keep on smell - ing Old men's macs Or when my ears are
or when I re - mem - ber How I feel The day af - ter an
bove my head there flies a Jum - bo Jet When all my towels are
wash up din - ner but I Get no thanks When - ev - er I smell
Dm7 G C Gm6 A7sus A7
blocked with wax Or con - ver - sa - tion turns to
In - dian meal Or when I see a jel - lied
drip - ping wet Or when my pink blanc - mange won't
sep - tic tanks When - ev - er I see two short
Dm Fm6 G7 G C E
To Coda
1.3.
tax - i - der - my I will think of you.
eel My dar - ling, I will think of
set My dar - ling, I will think of you.
planks My dar - ling, I will
Am Fm6 C G C G

2
a bit faster
you. Or when my best friend does - n't like
C9
Gm/C
Gm+/C
Be - ryl Cook or Da - vid Hock - ney
Or when I think of Dick van
C7
Fmaj7
F6
Fmaj7
F6
Fmaj7
F6
3
rall.
D.𝄋. al Coda
Dyke Try - ing to do a cock - ney ac - cent.
D7
F/G
Em/G
F/G
G13
CODA
Slower
think of you.
C
G
C
C

Funny How Things Turn Out

This song is very long and hard to remember. One of the penalties of being a solo performer is that when you go blank there's no-one to say 'I think I know what you're about to tell me, Colonel Pinky, Moira was seen in the shrubbery just after cocoa'. So when I dry up, it's just embarrassing and there's no way round it. In fact I've gone red now, just thinking about it. But that's one of the advantages of writing a book, you can't see me. Good job, because I've got a horrible T-shirt on.

Of all the letters that make me ill,
The rates demand, the telephone bill,
The ones that bring me really low
Are the ones from girls I used to know.
The girls at school you didn't like much
Have a terrible urge to keep in touch.
Those of whom you were not fond,
Relentlessly wield the Basildon Bond.

Remember Bobbie Field?
I won the Drama Shield.
An embryo actress and terribly thin.
Very ambitious, determined to win.
Auditioned for RADA and didn't get in.
Funny how things turn out.

I got my Equity card.
But the life was awfully hard.
I advertised cat-food for years which was hell.
Did 'Equus' at Windsor, which didn't go well.
And I asked for my key at the Crossroads Motel.
Funny how things turn out.

Though my kids are three, four and five.
I still keep my brain alive.
I've started to write, and I'm making some headway,
With humorous verses for Radio Medway,
My faith in myself is still devout.
Whenever I find I've a minute to kill,
I drive to the hospital up on the hill,
And sing Lerner and Lowe to the mentally ill.
Funny how things turn out.

Remember Jennifer Hill?
I was the first on the pill.
A bit of a hippie, and into 'tie-dye'
Trekked to Morocco, got ever so high.
Then I married a man from ICI
Funny how things turn out.

We moved to Tufnell Park
With a cat called Muriel Spark
I came off the pill 'cos it made me depressed
I hated the cap and the coil and the rest.
So I've three in the infants and two on the breast .
Funny how things turn out.

Now I sit from dawn to dusk
Covered in snot and Farley's Rusk.
I look back on the days of my youth and my passion
Wishing that loon-pants would come back in fashion.
And wondering what it's all about.
The doctor's advice has been largely ignored.
We did try the sheath but we got very bored.
So I'm writing to you from the Labour Ward.
Funny how things turn out.

Remember Brenda James?
I was Captain of Games.
I practised all day till my muscles were sore.
Hockey was super and boys were a bore.
Didn't use tampax till 'seventy-four.
Funny how things turn out.

At College I read sport.
But socially things were fraught.
I refused to have sex with a man called Des
He went around calling me 'Brenda the Les'
So I slept with a girl in my hall of res.
Funny how things turn out.

I 'came out' at a Lesbians Ball.
Didn't feel 'glad to be gay' at all.
Whoever said that, Tom Robinson, was it?
I couldn't agree and got back in the closet.
Then saw the light and had no doubt.
I took all my savings and just disappeared.
And found a nice doctor who said, 'You're not weird',
Now I'm Jonathan James with a wonderful beard
Funny how things turn out.

Funny How Things Turn Out

f
Cm G7 Cm
G7 Cm G7 Ab G
Of all the let-ters that make me ill, The rates de-mand, the tel-e-phone bill, The
Fm7 Bb7 Ebmaj7 Eb7 D7 G7
ones that bring me real - ly low Are the ones from girls I used to know. The
Cm G7 Ab G
girls at school you did - n't like much Have a ter - ri - ble ha - bit of keep-ing in touch.

Slower
Those of whom you were not fond, Re - lent - less - ly wield the Bas - il - don Bond. Re -
C7 Bb Cm7b5 C7 F Gm7 F° F Bb Cm7 Bb° Bb
a tempo
SPOKEN
mem - ber Bob - bie Field? I won the Dra - ma Shield. An
mem - ber Jen - ni - fer Hill I was the first on the pill. A
mem - ber Bren - da James? I was Cap - tain of Games. I
Eb Bb Eb Ab Bb Eb
em - bry - o ac - tress and ter - ri - bly thin. Ve - ry am - bi - tious, de - ter - mined to win. Au -
bit of a hip - pie, and in - to 'tie - dye'. Trekked to Mo - roc - co, got ev - er so high. Then I
prac - tised all day till my mus - cles were sore. Hock - ey was su - per and boys were a bore.
Eb G7 Cm7 F7 Bb7
di - tioned for RA DA but did - n't get in
mar - ried a man from I C I
Did - n't use Tam - pax till 'se - ven - ty - four.
Fun - ny how things turn out.
I
We
At
Eb Eb7 Abmaj7 Abm Eb Bb7 Eb Bb9

got my E - qui - ty card. But the life was aw - ful - ly hard. I
moved to Tuf - nell Park With a cat called Mu - ri - el Spark I
Col - lege I___ read sport. But social - ly things were fraught. I re -
Eb Bb Eb Ab Bb Eb
ad - ver - tised cat - food for years which was hell. Did 'E-quus' at Wind-sor, which did - n't go well. And I
came off the pill 'cos it made me de - pressed I ha-ted the cap and the coil and the rest. So I've
fused to have sex with a man called Des He went round call - ing me 'Bren - da the Les' So I
Eb G7 Cm7 F7 Bb7
asked for my key at the Cross-roads Mo - tel.
three in the in - fants and two on the breast.
slept with a girl in my hall of res.
Fun - ny how things turn out.
Eb Eb7 Abmaj7 Abm Eb Bb7 Eb G7
Though my kids___ are three, four and five, Still I keep my brain a - live I've
Now I sit___ from dawn to dusk Covered in snot and Far - ley's Rusk. I look
I 'came out'___ at a Les - bi - ans Ball. Didn't feel 'glad to be gay' at all.
Cm G7 Ab G

start - ed to write and I'm mak-ing some head-way, With hu-mo-rous vers - es for Ra - di - o Med - way, My
back on the days of my youth and my pas - sion Wish-ing that loon-pants would come back in fash-ion. And
Who - ev - er said that, Tom Ro - bin - son, was it? I could-n't a - gree and got back in the clo - set.
Fm7 Bb7 Ebmaj7 Eb7 Fm Dm7 G7 C7
faith in my-self is still de - vout. When - ev - er I find I've a min-ute to kill, I
won - der - ing what it's all a - bout. The doc-tor's ad-vice has been large-ly ig - nored. We
Then saw the light and had no doubt. I took all my sa - vings and just dis - ap-peared And
F9 Bb Ab/Bb Gm/Bb Bb7 Eb G7
drive to the hos - pi - tal up on the hill and sing Ler - ner and Loewe to the men-tal - ly ill.
did try the sheath but we got ve - ry bored. So I'm writ - ing to you from the La - bour Ward.
found a nice doc - tor who said "You're not weird". Now I'm Jo - na - than James with a won-der-ful beard.
C7 F9
1.2.
Fun-ny how things turn out. Re -
3
Fun-ny how things turn out.
Bb7 Eb C7 F13 Bb13 Bb7 Eb

I first sang this song with Julie in 'Wood and Walters'. She walked about and I did the harmony. She sang it in B flat but I do it in C because I'm two inches taller. We wore suits and someone wrote in and said she looked like Bobby Ball and I looked like Harold Wilson. Somebody else said I looked like a bag of laundry. It was my sister.

'Don't do it', is quite a hard song to remember because all the choruses begin with the same words. It's easy to muddle them up, and then you've got people taking overdoses before they've even got miserable.

Don't Do It

Don't Do It

Slow
She mar - ried ear - ly Was the thing to do
sank when she saw him he smelled of smoke She
Friends round for cof - fee Near - ly ev - 'ry day She was
Cm9
Fsus
F
Smiled for the pho - tos Like a dream come true He said he'd
knew ev - 'ry move-ment She'd heard ev - 'ry joke They made
smil - ing and des -perate But didn't like to say Count - ed
Cm9
Cm
Fmsus
Fm
love her for ev - er As if. It's a
love with the light off And no - thing said And the
pills in a bot - tle And dared her - self Heard his
Fm7
Bb7
Eb9
Eb
shame he ne - ver pro - mised Not to bore her stiff.
thought that she could change things Ne - ver en - tered her head.
car stop in the drive - way Put them back on the shelf.
Ab7
G7

Moderate bounce
On - ly the lone - ly would ev - er dis - pute what I'm say - ing
Cm
Cm(#7)
Cm7
Cm6
Fm9
Take it or leave it you'd bet - ter be - lieve what I'm
G7
Cm
Cm(#7)
Cm7
Cm6
say - ing
1. It is a crime to be stuck by the
2. Why should you miss out on laugh - ter on
3. Why bo - ther smil - ing in pub - lic and
Fm9
B♭
Cm7
B♭
E♭
B♭7
side of a per - son You don't ev - en like, tell me what could be worse than A
joy and e - la - tion? Un - less you are count - ing on re - in - car - na - tion It's
pri - vate - ly schem - ing? You're bet - ter off shout - ing and kick - ing and scream - ing It's
E♭7
A♭
A♭m7

To Coda
life full of no - thing? It's stu - pid, it's pain - ful.
one life and one chance It's ea - si - ly ru - ined.
soft to give in, to give up To go un - der.
Don't do it
Eb G7 C7 F7 Bb
CODA
Her heart
She had
Don't do it
Eb G7(#9) F7 Bb7
Cm Cm(#7) Cm7 Cm6 Fm9
Don't do it.
G7 Cm Cm(#7) Cm7 Cm6

Why bo - ther smil - ing in pub - lic and
pri - vate - ly sche - ming You're bet - ter off shout - ing and kick - ing and scream - ing it's
soft to give in, to give up to go un - der. Don't do it
Fm9
Bb
Cm7
Bb
Eb
Bb7
Eb7
Ab
Abm7
E
G7
C7
F7
Bb7
Cm
Cm(#7)
Cm7
Cm6
Fm9
G7(#9)
Cm9
C

Don't Do It

1. She married early.
   Was the thing to do.
   Smiled for the photos.
   Like a dream come true.
   He said he'd love her for ever.
   As if.
   It's a shame he never promised
   Not to bore her stiff.

   Only the lonely would ever dispute what I'm saying
   Take it or leave it you'd better believe what I'm saying
   It is a crime to be stuck by the side of a person
   You don't even like, tell me what could be worse than
   A life full of nothing?
   It's stupid, it's painful,
   Don't do it.

2. Her heart sank when she saw him.
   He smelled of smoke.
   She knew every movement.
   She'd heard every joke.
   They made love with the light off.
   And nothing said.
   And the thought that she could change things
   Never entered her head.

   Only the lonely would ever dispute what I'm saying.
   Take it or leave it you'd better believe what I'm saying.
   Why should you miss out on laughter, on joy and elation?
   Unless you are counting on reincarnation,
   It's one life and one chance,
   It's easily ruined,
   Don't do it.

3. She had friends round for coffee,
   Nearly ever day.
   She was smiling and desperate,
   But didn't like to say.
   Counted pills in a bottle,
   And dared herself.
   Heard his car stop in the driveway,
   Put them back on the shelf.

   Only the lonely would ever dispute what I'm saying
   Take it or leave it you'd better believe what I'm saying.
   Why bother smiling in public and privately scheming?
   *You're better off shouting and kicking and screaming
   It's soft to give in, to give up,
   To go under,
   Don't do it.

   (Repeat from*)

What We Find

This is another one I wrote for 'Wood and Walters'. I first sang it at the Bolton Festival. I don't remember if it went well, though I can remember having a cheese and tomato pizza. I never have pizzas with lots of bits on. I'm very unadventurous. When I play 'Monopoly' I always buy the stations and the utilities. It was only about last year when I found out how to pronounce 'Marylebone'. I still don't like saying it to taxi drivers. I'd rather be dropped off on the Euston Road and walk.

What We Find

Moderately bright
mf
Time plays tricks On one and all Our
Swim for health You splash a - bout The
D9
A7
ends are split Our bos-oms fall Well this is Af - ter all What we
chlor - ine makes your hair fall out Serves you right This is it What we
Dmaj7
G9
D
Fm7(♭5)/A
find.
find.
Time and tide Let's not for - get Will
You rub your necks Be - fore you sleep With
A7sus
A7
D9
A7
kill you off Or get you wet Thus is it This is life Ne-ver
cream that's made from bits of sheep Is this wise? Are you mad? Is it
Dmaj7
G9
D
Fm7(♭5)/A

mind.
kind?
But
Be
some girls don't know when they're bea-ten
like the old girls down the lo-cal
They
All
A7sus
A7
Gm7
Dm
Am7
Dm
Am7
bat-tle like old King Ca-nute
hal-ter-neck, Crim-plene and gin
To
Red
give ev-'ry wrin-kle
lip-stick and den-tures
Each
They
Gm7
Dm
Am7
Dm
Am7
Gm7
C7
crow's foot and crin-kle
still have ad-ven-tures
The
Join
boot.
You
Fmaj7
B♭maj7
A7sus
A7
in.
get faster
You try sex with
A younger man
He's
A7sus
A7
C7
F
C7

ne-ver heard Of Steel-eye Span What a blow What a drag What we
F
B♭
F
Fm7(♭5)/C
find. As time moves on It leaves its clues The
C7sus
C7
F
C7
tramps are wear - ing Plat-form shoes. Time's wing-ed bus Is just one
F
B♭
F
step Be - hind. Oh
Fm7(♭5)/C
C7sus

please give up
This pain - ful fight
A - gainst grey hair
And
F
C7
F
cell - u - lite
Please en - joy
What you are
Ask me
Bb
F
Fo
how
Live for now
Live for now
C7sus
C7
F
Db
F
Live for now.
Db
Bb
F6

What We Find

Time plays tricks
On one and all
Our ends are split
Our bosoms fall.
Well this is
After all
What we find.

Time and tide,
Let's not forget
Will kill you off
Or get you wet
Thus it is
This is life
Never mind.

But some girls don't know when they're beaten.
They battle like old King Canute
To give every wrinkle
Each crow's foot and crinkle
The boot.

You swim for health
You splash about
The chlorine makes your hair fall out
Serves you right
This is it
What we find.

You rub your necks
Before you sleep
With cream that's made from bits of sheep
Is this wise?
Are you mad?
Is it kind?

Be like the old girls down the local
All halter-neck Crimplene, and gin.
Red lipstick and dentures
They still have adventures
Join in.

You try sex with
A younger man
He's never heard
Of Steeleye Span.
What a blow
What a drag
What we find.

As time moves on
It leaves its clues
The tramps are wearing
Platform shoes.
Time's winged bus
Is just one step
Behind.

Oh please give up
This painful fight
Against grey hair
And cellulite
Please enjoy
What you are
Ask me how.
Live for now
Live for now
Live for now.

Fourteen Again

I used to precede this song with a few jolly remarks about being drunk and leaning over washbasins, and that's when I found out how few people think 'Twyfords', is a funny word. Especially at the King's Head Theatre in Islington. It's a very nice theatre but this practice of giving people dinner before the show does rather lead them to think they're in their own homes. On Monday they would start off by putting their handbags on the stage, and by Saturday they were doing jigsaws on the tables, and shaving from the light sockets.

Fourteen Again

chif - fon scarf.
I want to be four - teen a - gain
F7sus F7 B♭ F7sus F7
Ta - ttoo my - self with a foun - tain pen,
Pre - tend to like the taste of rum and coke,
Fm7 B♭sus B♭ E♭ E♭m7
Chuck my school hat in a bush,
B♭ B♭+ B♭6 A7 D7 E♭9 D7 E♭9 D7
Spit on my mas - ca - ra brush, Buy Con - su - late and teach my - self to
G7 C7

smoke.
I want to be four - teen a-gain, Free
F7
F7
rides on the walt-zer off the fair - ground men For a pro-mise of a snog the last night of the
Bb
fair
French kiss-ing as the ki-osks shut Be - hind the gen-er-a-tors with your co-co-nut,
Fm7
Bb7
Eb
Ebm
Bb
Fm6
G7
slower
The col-oured lights re-flect-ed in the Bryl-creem on his hair.
I want to be four-teen a-gain
C7sus
C7
F7sus
F7
Bb
F7sus
F7

For all the things I did-n't know then. When I was funny, I was fa-mous, I was

Fm7 Bbsus Bb Eb Ebm

ne-ver ig - nored___ I was a cra - zy girl,___ I had a laugh, I had

Bb Bb° Cm7

Il - y - a Ku-(oo)-ri - a-kin's au - to-graph, I had no i - dea___ you could

Dm G7sus G7 C7sus C7

wake up feel-ing bored.___

F7sus F7 Bbmaj7 Cm7 F7 Bb6

Fourteen Again

I want to be fourteen again,
When sex was just called number ten,
And I was up to seven and a half.
Boys were for love, girls were for fun,
You burst out laughing if you saw a nun,
Sophistication was a sports car and a chiffon scarf.

I want to be fourteen again,
Tattoo myself with a fountain pen,
Pretend to like the taste of rum and coke,
Chuck my school hat in a bush,
Spit on my mascara brush,
Buy Consulate and teach myself to smoke.

I want to be fourteen again,
Free rides on the waltzer off the fairground men
For a promise of a snog the last night of the fair –
French kissing as the kiosks shut
Behind the generators with your coconut,
The coloured lights reflected in the Brylcream on his hair.

I want to be fourteen again
For all the things I didn't know then.
When I was funny, I was famous, I was never ignored,
I was a crazy girl, I had to laugh,
I had Ilya Kuriakin's autograph,
I had no idea you could wake up feeling bored.

Love Song

This is about the only sad song I do, so usually people aren't prepared for it. That's why the intro is so long, to give the audience a chance to stop laughing and get a bit bored. Sometimes people cry when they hear it. I can tell because when they come backstage and shake hands they've got snot on their sleeves. (I just made that up.) I wrote the song for a revue at the Bush Theatre called 'In at the Death'. There was a sketch set in Belfast and I couldn't do the accent, so they made me a deaf mute.

Love Song

Moderato
1
2
F9 F C9 C Dm Gsus G C
Made your break-fast this morn-ing Like an-y old day And then I re-
kiss you But you al-ways laughed And I want-ed to
Sur-gical By your bed I knew that I
C9 C F9 F Fmaj7 F6 C9 C Cmaj7 C6
mem-bered And threw it a-way. Found an old pho-to In the kit-chen
tell you But I felt daft. Still we got mar-ried I was
loved you But I nev-er said. I brought you Black Ma-gic And they said you'd
Dm7 Gsus G7 C9 Gm6 D7
drawer. You by the sea-side Dur-ing the war. You're laugh-ing at
tight. Then we both got em-bar-rassed Played rummy all night. I re-mem-ber the
died. I had a cup of tea there, Came home and cried. Got to go back to the
D9 Dm7 Dm7+ G7 C9 Gm6

some-thing And the winds in your hair You were ev - er so slim then And your hair was still
ba - by And its stick - y - out ears, But I can't sin - gle out things Ov - er the
hos-pi-tal To col-lect your things Your night - ie, your teeth And your wed-ding
A7
D9
Dm7 Dm7+ G7
1.2.
3
fair And I want-ed to ring. Made your break-fast this mor-ning Like an-y old day And then I re-
years. In Wo - men's
C9 C
C9 C
F9 F Fmaj7 F6
C9 C Cmaj7 C6
1
2
mem-bered And threw it a - way.__ Made you break-fast this __
Dm7 G7sus G7
C9 C
C9 C
rall.
F9 F
C9 C
Dm7 Gsus G C

Love Song

Made your breakfast this morning
Just like any old day,
And then I remembered
And I threw it away.

Found an old photo
In the kitchen drawer –
You by the seaside
During the war.
You're laughing at something
And the wind's in your hair.
You were ever so slim then,
And your hair was still fair.

And I wanted to kiss you
But you always laughed,
And I wanted to tell you
But I felt daft.

Still we got married,
I was tight.
Then we both got embarrassed
Played rummy all night.
I remember the baby
And its sticky-out ears,
But I can't single out things
Over the years.

In Women's Surgical
By your bed,
I knew that I loved you,
But I never said.
I brought you Black Magic,
And they said you'd died.
I had a cup of tea there,
Came home and cried.

Got to go back to the hospital
To collect your things –
Your nightie, your teeth
And your wedding ring.

Made your breakfast this morning
Just like any old day,
And then I remembered
And I threw it away.
Made you breakfast this morning
Just like any old day,
And then I remembered
And I threw it away.

Nasty Things

This song was written for the comedienne and vocaliste Paula du Val, by that reasonably well-known song-writing duo, Betty and Derek Dewsbury. They've written many fabulous melodies for Paula, including 'Well, it's just not good enough, our Glynis', and the very popular ballad 'I'm snip-snip-snipping his toenails, but I can't do the one on the left.'

1. There's nasty things wherever you look
   There's nasty things in every book
   You're down and out
   You've got no rent
   Your leg's been mashed in an accident.
   There's nasty things wherever you look.

2. There's nasty things wherever you go
   There's nasty folks around, and I know.
   They offer you life's brimming cup
   Then they make you puke it up.
   There's nasty things wherever you go.

Chorus. Grease and grime
Sludge and slime
Evil doing and skulduggery
Do we fight
To put them right
Let's face it, do we buggery.

3. There's nasty things all over in life
   There's nasty things in being a wife
   You make things nice
   But does he care
   Keeps maggots in your Tupperware.
   There's nasty things all over in life.

Chorus. If life's a boat
Then mine don't float.
My oars come out my rowlocks.
You say, not at all
Life's a ball
Then my reply is – arseholes.

4. There's nasty things whatever you do
   There's nasty things just waiting for you.
   At the pearly gates
   You make your bow
   They say: – heaven's shut – it's Bingo now.
   There's nasty things whatever you do.

Nasty Things

1st time D.𝄋.
2nd & 3rd to Chorus
There's nas - ty things wher - ev - er you look.
There's nas - ty things wher - ev - er you go.
There's nas - ty things all ov - er in life.
If
G7
C
CHORUS
Grease and grime sludge and slime Ev - il do - ing
life's a boat Then mine don't float My oars come
C7
F
and skull dug-g'ry Do we fight To put them
out my row-locks. You say, not at all Life's a
D7
right? Let's face it do we bug - g'ry.
ball Then my re - ply is arse - holes.
G7
Cm6
G7

4. There's nas - ty things what - ev - er you do
C
G7
C
There's nas - ty things just wait - ing for you.
Slower
At the
Am
E7
Am
pear - ly gates You make your bow They say: Hea - ven's shut it's Bin - go now.
a tempo 1º
Dm
Ab7
C
D7
There's nas - ty things what - ev - er you do.
G7
C B Eb A Ab G7 C

The Song of the Lonely Girl

This is a little number Brecht and Weill forgot to write. It was inspired by seeing two girls in belted raincoats and plenty of lipstick perform a non-stop medley of Brecht songs. It was the sort of evening in the theatre where you find yourself wondering what your tea-towels would come out like if you dyed them.

I knew a girl
A lonely girl
Who could not get her hair to curl
Who'd never had a man
(She wanted a man)
And every night she'd take her pill
Put on that stuff called Clearasil
And plan herself a little plan.

She would say
Please, I want a lover
Someone to cover me with kisses
Till I've had my fill.
He must be gentle
And sentimental
And he must possess a Black and
Decker drill.

God sent her William from Wembley
He was into self-assembly
He put wardrobes up for fun
(Not my cup of tea)
He would laugh with her and cry with
her
He went to M F I with her
What more could he have done?

But she said
No, I want a poet
Whose love will show itself to me,
Whose words will make it clear
He must be arty,
Make life a party.
And he must come out in paperback
this year.

God sent her Tom, an intellectual
In bed, quite ineffectual.
Not even very bright
(Poor Tom)
Not only was he not erect
He wrote monologues in dialect.
And read them out aloud all night.

So she said
Please, send someone hunky
He must be chunky with a tan
And sexy deep blue eyes.
Let muscles ripple
From knee to nipple.
And I think I'll let the rest be a
surprise.

God sent her Dave, whose wonderful
physique
Resulted from a six day week
At the Y M C A.
(What more is there to say?)
She stayed the night, but all he'd
show
Was Bette Davis on the video.
When morning came she sadly walked
away.

That lonely girl came off the pill
Gave up that stuff called Clearasil.
It's sad don't you agree,
(Quite sad)
But she's OK, she gets along.
She tells a joke, she sings a song.
Ah yes, because that girl was me.

The Song of the Lonely Girl

To Coda
poco rall.
(8va ad lib.
on that stuff called Clear - a - sil And plan her - self a lit - tle
went to M F I with her What more could he have
mon - o - logues in di - a - lect. And read them out a - loud all
Bet - te Da - vis on the vi - de - o. When mor - ning came she sad - ly walked a -
Ab F B7 C B7
plan. She would say Please, I want a lov - er Some-one to
done? But she said No, I want a po - et Whose love will
night. So she said Please, send some - one hun - ky He must be
Em Em7 Am7 D7 Gmaj7 Cmaj7
co - ver me with kiss - es Till I've had my fill. He must be gen - tle And sen - ti -
show it - self to me, Whose words will make it clear He must be ar - ty, Make life a
chunk - y with a tan And sex - y deep blue eyes. Let mus - cles rip - ple From knee to
F♯m7 D7 rall. E E7 Am7 D7
1.2.3.
men - tal And he must pos - sess a Black and Deck - er drill. God sent her
par - ty And he must come out in pa - per - back this year. God sent her
nip - ple. And I think I'll let the rest be a sur - prise. God sent her
Gmaj7 Cmaj7 Am6 B7

CODA
way.
That lone - ly girl came off the pill Gave
Em
Am6
C7
B7
Em
C
up that stuff called Clear - a - sil.
It's sad don't you a - gree?
(Quite
A
F
B7
Am
sad)
But she's O K, she gets a - long, She tells a joke, she sings a song.
Ah
B7
Am
B7
Em
C
Ab
F
8va ad lib.
yes, be - cause that girl was me.
B7
C
B7
Em
Am6
C7
B7
Em

I've Had It Up to Here

What can I say about this song, except that on the nights it goes really well, I know I'm not going to get any laughs with 'Music and Movement'. It's out of a musical I wrote called 'Good Fun'. One reviewer described me as 'dominating the stage like a witty tank'. I was thinner then, but I had a very big anorak. In fact, for some matinees the anorak would go on by itself. It got more laughs but it couldn't play the piano. The play was about a cystitis rally, which led to lots of unpleasant correspondence with members of the public, who would write brief notes (well, they'd have to be brief, wouldn't they?) 'I've got cystitis and it isn't funny', to which I would reply 'Send it back and ask for one that is'. The trouble with this song is that people think I hate sex. I don't. I just don't like things that stop you seeing the television properly.

I've Had It Up to Here

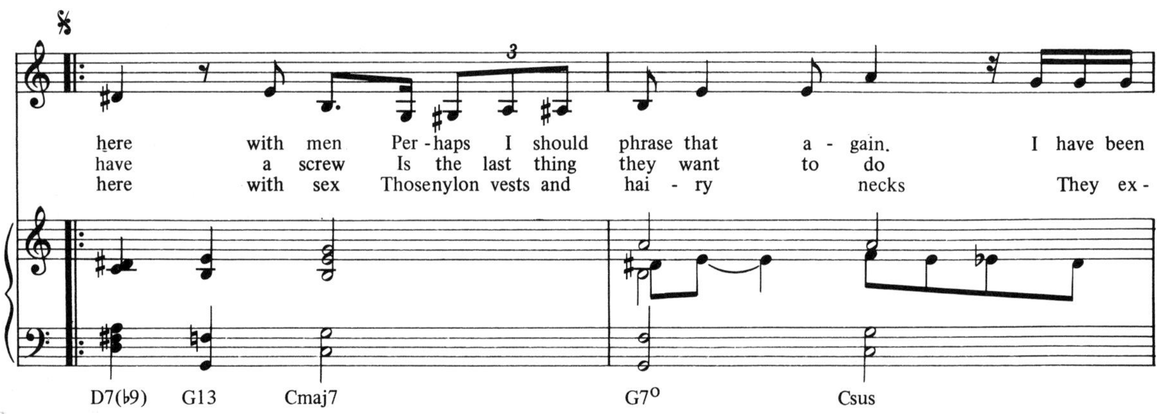

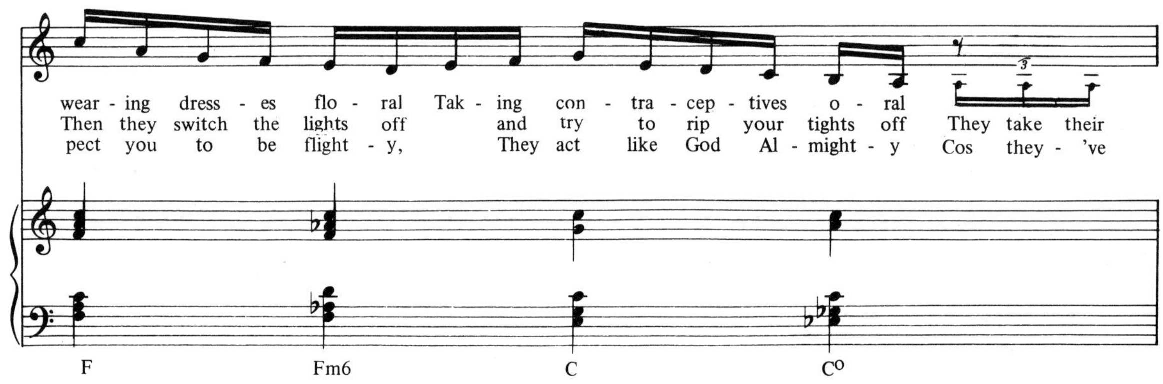

Since I don't re - mem - ber when. I've had it up to
cof - fee with su - gar, milk and you. It's not that I ex -
got a cock and they can mend a flex, When they proud - ly
Dm7
G7+
here with blokes And all their stu - pid dir - ty jokes It's
pect true love or ga - zing at the stars a - bove If as a
strip and pose, I want to say 'What's one of those?' They
D7(♭9)
G13
Cmaj7
G7+
Csus
1
not a lot of fun to hear the one a-bout the nun The mar-row the ba-na-na and John Noakes. Men act as if to
per-son they'd ack-now-ledge me Not bits of gyn - ae - co-lo-gy Or
tend to feel a fail - ure If you don't love their gen-i-ta-li - a Though
F
Fm6
C
C°
Dm7
G7+
2.3.
if they'd just take off the rub-ber glove. To start your ev-'ning off in Lur-ex And fin-ish it with bis-cuits
why you should God on - ly knows. No more nights of drinking, Nod-ding, smil-ing, think-ing,
Dm7
G13
C
B7
E
F♯m7
E°
E

Does-n't real-ly turn me on I'll stay at home in my py-ja-mas, Watch a pro-gramme a-bout lla-mas I
'Je-sus when can I go home?' No more stru-ggl-ing in ta-xis In Vaux-halls, Imps and Ma-xis With
E F♯m7 E° E F♯ G♯m7 F♯° F♯
won't need an-y lip gloss I won't need an-y Am-plex Just O-val-tine and buns for one. I've had it up to
stu - pid lit-tle blee-ders with all the charm-ing man-ners Of the
1
D.𝄋
B B♭+ F♯m A♭7 G13
2
3
av - er - age gar - den gnome. And when they're down to socks and grin you know it's time to
F♯m A♭7 G13 D7(♭9) G13 Cmaj7
get stuck in. Full of self con-gra - tu - la - tion They ex-pect a com-bi - na-tion Of Ol - ga
3
G7° Csus F Fm6 C C°

Kor-but, Ra-quel Welch and Rin-Tin-Tin, I've not had an en-coun - ter yet That did-n't leave me
Dm7
G7+
D7(♭9)
G13
Cmaj7
cold and wet I'd be hap-pi-er I know If we could on-ly go from the
G7+
Csus
F
Fm6
3
fore-play straight to the ci-gar-ette. I'll fin-ish and just say a - gain I've
Dm7
D♭maj7
G7+
C
de-fin-ite-ly had it, Well ve-ry near-ly had it, Had it near-ly up to here with men.
C
B7
Gm6
A7
Dm7
G13
C

I've Had It Up to Here

I've had it up to here with men –
Perhaps I should phrase that again.
Been wearing dresses, floral,
Taking contraceptives (oral),
Since I don't remember when.
I've had it up to here with blokes,
And all their stupid dirty jokes
It's not a lot of fun
To hear the one about the nun
The marrow, the banana and John Noakes.

Men act as if to have a screw
Is the last thing they want to do.
Then they switch the lights off
And try and rip your tights off,
They take their coffee with sugar, milk and you.
It's not that I expect true love,
Or gazing at the stars above –
If as a person, they'd acknowledge me,
Not bits of gynaecology,
Or if they'd just take off the rubber glove.

To start your evening off in Lurex,
And finish it with biscuits
Doesn't really turn me on.
I'll stay at home in my pyjamas,
Watch a programme about llamas,
I won't need any lip-gloss,
I won't need any Amplex,
Just Ovaltine and buns for one.

I've had it up to here with sex,
Those nylon vests and hairy necks.
They expect you to be flighty,
They act like God Almighty,
'Cos they've got a cock, and they can mend a flex.
When they proudly strip and pose,
I want to say 'What's one of those?'
They tend to feel a failure
If you don't love their genitalia,
Though why you should, God only knows.

No more nights of drinking,
Nodding, smiling, thinking
'Jesus, when can I go home?'
No more struggling in taxis,
In Vauxhalls, Imps and Maxis
With stupid little bleeders
With all the charming manners
Of the average garden gnome.

And when they're down to socks and grin,
You know it's time to get stuck in.
Full of self-congratulation,
They expect a combination
Of Olga Korbut, Raquel Welch
And Rin-Tin-Tin.
I've not had an encounter yet
That didn't leave me cold and wet.
I'd be happier, I know,
If we could only go
From the foreplay straight to the cigarette.

I'll finish and just say again
I've definitely had it,
Well very nearly had it,
Had it nearly up to here with men.

Bastards

I must confess I've used this tune once before, for an education programme. It was a long time ago, before I had my hair cut anyway. I have it cut quite a lot now, and what I want to know is, are you supposed to tip the woman who brings you the cup of tea? The whole operation is fraught with potential embarrassments, let alone the fact that you are stuck for three hours reading *House and Garden*.

Outside, I'm desperate to please.
I say the things you want to hear, I'm kind.
I don't complain to waiters, I'm keen to be well-liked
I smile a lot and never speak my mind.

But inside, I'm bursting with ill-will.
And one day the veneer will start to crack.
First I'll stop the smiling, and then the little lies
And maybe I'll go mad and answer back.

Whenever they say
Are you happy with your hair?
I'll say I think the perm was a mistake.
It looks absolutely foul
The best bit is the towel
I refuse to pay to look like Charlie Drake.

Whenever he says
How was it for you?
I'm going to say, it was not good enough.
It makes a cervical smear
Seem like a good idea.
And by the way, your navel's full of fluff.

Whenever they say
Did you enjoy the meal?
I'll say, your waiter has a CSE in sloth.
The soup was freezing cold
And the strawberries had mould
And the coq-au-vin reminded me of both.

Whenever they cry
Well aren't we having fun,
Barbara's parties always go so well?
I'll say, I'm bored out of my brains
I've had more fun down the drains
I'm going to slash my wrists or read *The White Hotel.*

And when the bastards say
Did you enjoy the show?
I'll say I did not like it, it was crap.
I was really really bored
It should win a fringe award.
They had to wake me up to make me clap.

So whatever they say
Just say something back
It's time the social liars went on strike.
Truth is just the job
Make trouble with your gob.
You just tell them what the hell, yes
You just tell them what the hell, yes
You just tell them what the hell you like.

Bastards

Bright
f
Fm7
Bb♭m9 Bb♭m7 Bb♭m9 Bb♭m7
Fm9 Fm7 Fm7 Bb♭m7 Bb♭m7
Out - side__ I'm des-per - ate__ to please. I
in - side__ I'm burst-ing with_ ill- will. And
say the things you want to hear,_ I'm kind.____
one day the ve- neer will start__ to crack.____
I don't com-plain to wait-ers, I'm
First I'll stop the smi-ling, and
3
Bb♭m9 Fm9 Bb♭m7 Eb♭7
keen to be well liked I smile a lot and nev- er speak my mind.____ But
then the lit - tle lies And may - be I'll go mad and an- swer
1
Ab♭maj7 Db♭maj7 Bb♭m6 Gb♭maj7 Gm7/C C7

2

back.

1. When - ev - er they say Are you
2. When - ev - er he says
4. When - ev - er they cry Well
5. And when the bas-tards say Did

Gm7/C C7 Gm7 C7 Gm9/C

hap - py with your hair? I'll say I think the perm was a mis - take. It looks
How was it for you? I'm going to say it was not good e - nough. It
aren't we hav - ing fun, Bar- bara's par - ties al- ways go so well? I'll say I'm
you en - joy the show? I'll say I did not like it, it was crap. I was

F9 Gm9 F9

ab - so - lute - ly foul The best bit is the towel I re - fuse to pay to look like Char - lie
made a cer- vical smear Seem like a good i - dea. And by the way, your na - vel's full of
bored out of my brains I've had more fun down drains I'm going to slash my wrists or read 'The White Ho -
real - ly real - ly bored It should win a fringe a - ward. They had to wake me up to make me

A7sus A7 Dm7 G7sus G7

Drake.
fluff.
tel.'
clap.

3. When-ev - er they say Did you en - joy the meal? I'll say your
6. So what-ev-er they say Just say some-thing back It's

C9 Gm7/C F9

wait - er has a C S E in sloth
time the so - cial li - ars went on strike.
The soup was freez-ing cold And the
Truth is just the job Make
Gm9
A7 Bm7 A° A Dm7
To Coda ⊕
straw- ber - ries had mould And the coq - au - vin re - mind - ed me of both.
trou - ble with your gob.
G7
Gm7 C7 F F°
D.%. al Coda with Repeat
⊕ CODA
You just tell them what the hell, yes You just tell them what the hell, yes
F Gm7
Gm7
You just tell them what the hell you like.
Gm7 C7 F F° Gm9 F6

Music and Movement

It's bad enough at school without the wireless
We have it nearly every afternoon.
It's something called Music and Movement
When you run about to a tune.

I wouldn't mind if it was cops and robbers
But the lady tells you what you have to be
And I'm only a mixed infant
So it isn't up to me.

And now we're in the hall with the wireless on
With this woman saying what we have to do.
Be as tall as a house
As tiny as a mouse
I'm knackered and it's only half past two.

It's been a horrible day at school so far
My best friend didn't come
And I got demoted from milk monitor
'Cos they heard me saying bum.

And then I got in trouble in the playground
Had the slipper twice off Mrs Stock
'Cos Linda Morris tried to kiss me
And I put my wellie down her frock.

And now we're in the hall with the wireless on
Going on and on, we haven't had a rest
Pretend the day is sunny
You're a funny little bunny.
Have you ever seen a rabbit in a vest?

I'm making this Christmas tree out of lolly sticks
To take home to my mum.
But it's gone all crumply and sticky
'Cos I'm not very good with gum.

And shepherd's pie and cabbage for dinner
And it wasn't even hot
Spotted dick and custard
All dick and not a lot of spot.

And now we're in the hall with the wireless on
Our teacher's joining in, she's gone all red.
She's the moon and we're the sea
There's a big scab on my knee.
I'll save it for tonight when I'm in bed.

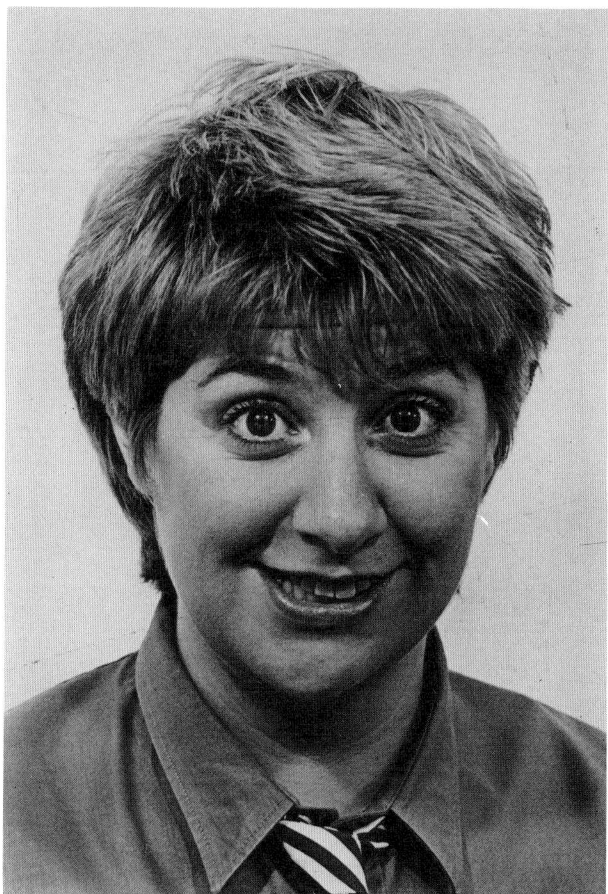

This is a very old song, but so many people seem to like it. I keep on doing it. Because it's the last song in the show I sometimes relax a little, and I have been known to go straight from the first verse to the last chorus, and find myself in the dressing room with my socks off, thinking 'What?'.

I wrote it for a radio programme produced by Alfred Bradley. We recorded it on a Sunday in Manchester, which is the only time I've ever been able to find a free meter.

I'm glad this song is in the book, because it means people won't need to write and ask me for the lyrics. I can't send them because I write everything in longhand, and I don't cross my t's, so 'there' looks like 'here'. Good job I didn't write 'Here, There and Everywhere', I suppose.

Music and Movement

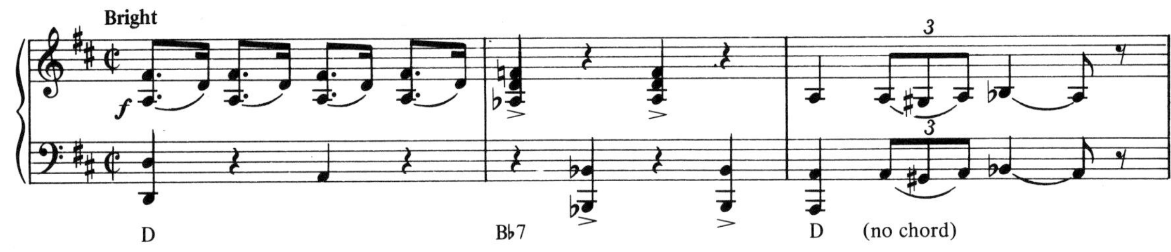
Bright
D
B♭7
D (no chord)

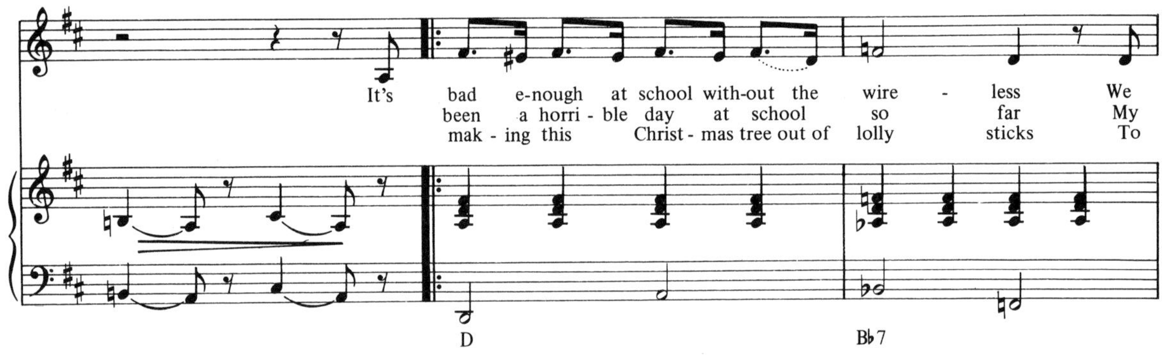
It's bad e-nough at school with-out the wire - less We
been a horri - ble day at school so far My
mak - ing this Christ - mas tree out of lolly sticks To
D
B♭7

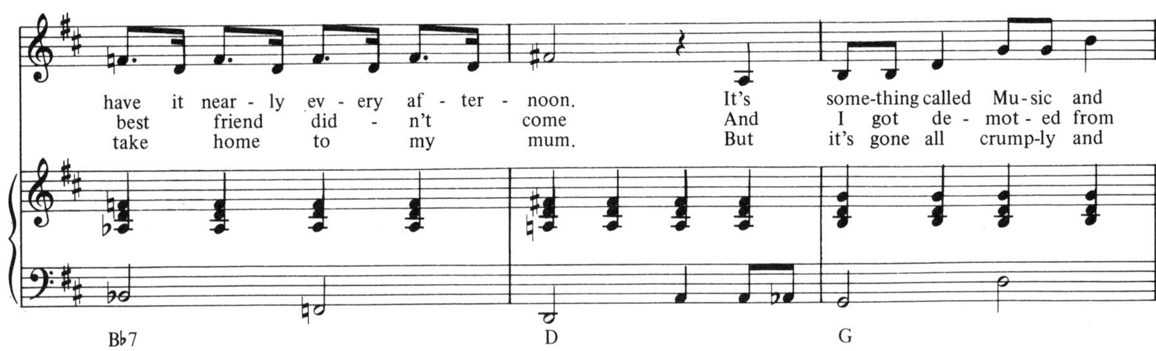
have it near - ly ev - ery af - ter - noon. It's some-thing called Mu-sic and
best friend did - n't come And I got de - mot - ed from
take home to my mum. But it's gone all crump-ly and
B♭7
D
G

Move - ment Where you run a - bout to a tune. I
milk monitor 'Cos they heard me say - ing bum. And
stick - y 'Cos I'm not very good with gum. And
D
E
A7
would - n't mind if it was cops and rob - bers But the la - dy tells you what you have to
then I got in troub - le in the play - ground Had the slip - per twice off Mr - s
shep - herd's pie and cab - bage for din - ner And it was - n't ev - en
D
B♭7
be And I'm on - ly a mixed in - fant So it
Stock 'Cos Linda Morris tried to kiss me And I
hot And spot - ted dick and cus - tard All
D
G
B7
E7
is - n't up to me. And
I put my welly down her frock. And
dick and not a lot of spot. And
3
3
A7
D
(no chord)

now we're in the hall with the wire - less on With this
now we're in the hall with the wire - less on Go - ing
now we're in the hall with the wire - less on Our
A7
wo - man say - ing what we have to do. Be as tall as a house Be as
on and on, we have - n't had a rest Pre - tend the day is sunny Be a
tea - chers join - ing in, she's gone all red. She's the moon and we're the sea There's a
D E7 A7sus A7 D D7
ti - ny as a mouse I'm knack - ered and it's on - ly half past
fun - ny lit - tle bunny. Have you ev - er seen a rab - bit in a
big scab on my knee. I'll save it for to - night when I'm in
Bm7 Bb7 D A7
1.2.
3
two. It's
vest? I'm
bed.
D (no chord) D A7 D

Northerners

There are a few professional Northerners about and I'm trying not to be one of them. That's why I wrote the song. We did it on 'Wood and Walters', with the actor Robert Longden giving an enthusiastic performance on the washboard. In fact all the ends of his fingers came off.

As a singer life was hell
I never did too well
I was never asked to play the same place twice
I was paid my final wage
Then an agent came backstage
And gave me some brilliant advice.

Pretend to be Northern
Just smile and act dense.
Just sing something Northern
It doesn't have to make sense.
Make a list of Northern clichés
And you can't go wrong
Put in any order
You've got a Northern song.

You just go:
Tripe, clogs
Going to the dogs
Wigan and Blackpool tram
Brass bands
Butties in your hands
Whippets and next door's mam.
Cloth cap
Hankie full of snap
Shawls and scabby knees
Hot-pot
Seven to a cot
Headscarves and mushy peas.

I threw away my skin-tight suits
And I brought some heavy boots
And I wore a woolly shawl all nice and flowery
I spent neet after neet
Watching Coronation Street
And studying the works of L.S. Lowry.

Now I'm fully Northern
And it works a treat
Spend half the year in Preston
And the other in Crete.
Buying a bungalow in Weybridge
Before too long
Once I've made enough brass
From my Northern song.

I just go:
Rag man
Eating out the pan
Tanners and threepenny bits
Prawn wheels
Good old Gracie Fields
Braces bugs and nits.
Fish, chips
Cycle chips
Gaslight and games in t'street
Nutty slack
Privy out the back
Gradely aye and reet.

Fog, smog
Sitting on the bog
Cobbles in the morning mist
Park Drive
Dead at forty-five
From a back street abortionist
(It's terrible).

Northerners

North - ern Just smile and act dense. Just sing some-thing
North - ern And it works a treat Spend half the year in
C G7
North - ern It does-n't have to make sense. Make a list of North-ern
Pres - ton And the oth - er in Crete. Buying a bun - ga - low in
C
cli - chés And you can't go wrong Put in an - y
Wey - bridge Be - fore too long Once I've made e -
C7 F Fm
or - der You've got a North - ern song. You just go
nough brass From my North - ern song. I just go
C Gsus G C G D7 G7

1st Time Slow and accel.
3rd and 4th Times getting fast
1. Tripe, clogs Go - ing to the dogs Wi - gan and Black - pool tram
Cloth cap Han - kie full of snap Shawls and scab - by knees
2. Rag man Eat - ing out the pan Tan - ners and three - penny bits
Fish, chips Cy - cle clips Gas - light and games in t' street
C
Brass bands But - ties in your hands Whippets and next door's mam.
Hot - pot Se - ven in a cot Head - scarves and mushy peas.
Prawn wheels Good old Gra - cie Fields Bra - ces bugs and nits.
Nutty slack Pri - vy out the back Grade - ly aye and reet.
G
1.3.
2
Tempo 1o
D.S. 𝄋.
2. I threw a -
C G D7 G7 C B7
4
Still Faster
Fog, smog Sit - ting on the bog
C G D7 G7 C C

Cob - bles in the mor - ning mist
Park Drive
C
G7
Spoken
Dead at for - ty - five From a back street a - bor - tion - ist (It's ter - ri - ble).
C
Hummed
C
E
Dm
Fm6
C
A7
D7
G7
C

Index of Song Titles

Bastards **65**

Don't Do It **29**

Don't Get Cocky **11**

Fourteen Again **41**

Funny How Things Turn Out **23**

I've Had It Up to Here **59**

Living Together **15**

Love Song **47**

Music and Movement **69**

Nasty Things **51**

Northerners **73**

The Song of the Lonely Girl **55**

Thinking of You **19**

What We Find **35**